PILOT

BOOK FOR SMART KIDS

How to Become a Pilot and Succeed in Aviation

MARTY HODGEF

Copyright © 2022 MARTY HODGEF

All rights reserved.

TABLE OF CONTENTS

INTRODUCTION 5

The History of Aviation 11

Airplanes 15

The Life of a Pilot 25

A Flight from Start to Finish 29

The Different Types of Pilots 35

The Essential Skills of a Pilot 41

Training and Education 49

Navigation and Flight Planning 55

Safety and Emergency Procedures 59

Air Traffic Control and Communication 63

Aircraft Systems and Maintenance 67

From School to Skies 73

Careers in Aviation 79

The Rewards 83

The Challenges 89

Tips for Success 95

CONCLUSION 99

MARTY HODGEF

INTRODUCTION

Have you ever looked up at the sky and watched an airplane soaring through the clouds, wondering what it would be like to be the person flying that plane? The world of aviation is an exciting and dynamic one, filled with adventure and opportunities to explore the world from a whole new perspective. In this book, we will take an in-depth look at what it takes to become a pilot and achieve success in your aviation career.

We will start by exploring the history of aviation, delving into the early pioneers of flight and how their innovations have shaped the industry into what it is today. You will learn about the different types of pilots, from commercial airline pilots to military fighter pilots, and the roles they play in the aviation industry. We will also take a look at the training and education required to become a pilot, including flight schools and the various certifications needed.

You will also learn about the day-to-day life of a pilot, including the responsibilities and challenges they face. Navigation and flight planning is a crucial aspect of being a pilot, and we will delve into the tools and techniques used to plan and execute a safe flight. Safety is of the utmost importance in aviation, and you will learn about the procedures pilots follow in case of emergency, as well as the importance of regular aircraft maintenance to ensure a safe flight.

Air traffic control and communication is also an important aspect of being a pilot, and we will explore how pilots communicate with air traffic control and other aircraft during a flight. Understanding the different systems and components of an aircraft, as well as how they are maintained, is crucial for any aspiring pilot.

In addition to learning about the technical side of flying, you will also learn about the various career opportunities available in aviation, including commercial, military, and private flying. We will also provide tips and strategies for achieving success in an aviation career, including the importance of networking, perseverance, and continuous learning.

This book is designed for kids who are interested in aviation and want to learn more about what it takes to become a pilot. It's an exciting journey, and we can't wait to take it together! With this book, you will gain a deeper understanding of the aviation industry and be well-equipped to pursue your dream of becoming a pilot. So, let's get started and discover the world of aviation together!

PART 1: AVIATION

MARTY HODGEF

CHAPTER 1:

The History of Aviation

The history of aviation is a fascinating story of human ingenuity and determination. From the earliest attempts at flight to the development of the modern airplane, the evolution of flight has shaped the world we live in today. In this chapter, we will take a closer look at the history of aviation and how it has impacted the world.

1. Early Attempts at Flight

The history of aviation begins with the earliest attempts at flight, dating back to ancient civilizations. From the Chinese kite to the Greek and Roman flying machines, early inventors sought to develop a means of powered flight. However, it wasn't until the 15th century that the first successful gliders were built by Leonardo da Vinci and other inventors.

2. The Wright Brothers and the First Powered Flight

The first successful powered flight was made by Orville and Wilbur Wright on December 17, 1903. Using a biplane, the Wright brothers made four flights that day, the longest lasting 59 seconds and covering a distance of 852 feet. This breakthrough marked the beginning of the modern era of aviation.

3. The Development of the Airplane

The Wright brothers' invention of the airplane marked the beginning of rapid developments in aviation. In the years that followed, airplanes were improved upon with the addition of engines, wheels, and other features that made them more practical for transportation and warfare.

4. The Impact of Aviation on Society

The invention of the airplane has had a profound impact on society. The ability to fly has revolutionized transportation, making it possible to travel across the globe in a matter of hours. It has also played a significant role in warfare, as well as in the fields of science and medicine. Today, aviation continues to shape the world we live in, connecting people and cultures, facilitating global trade, and making the world a smaller place.

5. Conclusion

The history of aviation is a fascinating story of human ingenuity and determination. From the earliest attempts at flight to the development of the modern airplane, the evolution of flight has shaped the world we live in today. The Wright brothers' invention of the airplane marked the beginning of rapid developments in aviation, and the impact of aviation on society has been profound, revolutionizing transportation and playing a significant role in various fields.

CHAPTER 2:

Airplanes

Airplanes are one of the most fascinating and complex machines ever built by humans. They have the ability to fly at incredible speeds, take us to the farthest corners of the globe, and have enabled a vast array of industries and activities. In this chapter, we will take a closer look at some of the most interesting facts and information about airplanes, including their design, technology, performance, safety, and different types.

1. Design

Airplanes are designed to be as aerodynamic as possible, allowing them to fly through the air with minimal resistance. The shape of the fuselage, wings, and tail are carefully designed to achieve the right balance of lift, drag, and stability. The wings are designed to generate lift, while the tail provides stability and control. The design of an airplane also includes the powerplant, which can be either a turbine or propeller engine. Turbine engines are more efficient and powerful but also more expensive to operate than propeller engines.

2. Technology

Airplanes are equipped with a wide range of advanced technologies that allow them to fly safely and efficiently. These include navigation systems, communication systems, weather radar, and flight control systems. Navigation systems allow pilots to plot the course and track the location of the aircraft, while communication systems allow pilots to communicate with air traffic control and other aircraft. Weather radar systems allow pilots to detect and avoid bad weather, and flight control systems help pilots control the airplane during flight.

3. Performance

Airplanes are capable of flying at incredible speeds and altitudes. The fastest commercial airplane in the world is the Concorde, which could fly at speeds of up to 1,350 miles per hour. The highest altitude ever reached by a commercial airplane is 53,000 feet, while the highest altitude ever reached by a military airplane is 85,000 feet. The range of an airplane is the distance it can fly without refueling, and it varies depending on the type of airplane and the amount of fuel it can carry.

4. Safety

Safety is a top priority for the aviation industry. Airplanes are equipped with multiple safety systems and features, including emergency oxygen systems, fire suppression systems, and emergency exit routes. Additionally, pilots are required to undergo regular training and certification to ensure they are capable of handling a wide range of emergency situations. The Federal Aviation Administration (FAA) and other regulatory bodies set and enforce safety standards for airplanes and the aviation industry to ensure the safety of passengers, crew, and the general public.

5. Types of Airplanes

There are many different types of airplanes, each with their own unique characteristics and uses. Some of the most common types of airplanes include:

- **Single-engine propeller airplanes:** small, single-engine planes that are typically used for personal or light-duty commercial flights.
- **Multi-engine propeller airplanes:** larger planes that are used for a variety of purposes, including commercial flights, cargo transport, and air ambulance services.
- **Turboprop airplanes:** similar to multi-engine propeller airplanes, but with turbine engines that provide more power and efficiency.
- **Jet airplanes:** the most common type of commercial airplane, jet airplanes are powered by jet engines and are used for both short and long-haul flights.
- **Military airplanes:** designed and built specifically for military use, these planes are typically faster, more maneuverable, and more heavily armed than commercial airplanes.

6. Conclusion

In summary, this chapter covers everything you need to know about airplanes, including design, technology, performance, safety, and different types of airplanes. The design of an airplane includes the shape of the fuselage, wings, and tail, which are designed to achieve the right balance of lift, drag, and stability. The powerplant can be either a turbine or propeller engine. The technology used in airplanes includes navigation systems, communication systems, weather radar, and flight control systems. Airplanes are capable of flying at incredible speeds and altitudes, but safety is always a top priority for the aviation industry. There are many different types of airplanes, each with their own unique characteristics and uses, such as single-engine propeller airplanes, multi-engine propeller airplanes, turboprop airplanes, jet airplanes, and military airplanes. Understanding the design, technology, performance, safety, and different types of airplanes is important for anyone interested in the aviation industry.

MARTY HODGEF

PART 2: PILOTS

MARTY HODGEF

CHAPTER 3:

The Life of a Pilot

Being a pilot is an exciting and rewarding career, but it also comes with its own set of responsibilities and challenges. In this chapter, we will take a closer look at the life of a pilot, including a typical day in the life of a pilot and the responsibilities and challenges they face.

1. A typical day in the life of a pilot

A typical day for a pilot begins well before the flight, as they have to prepare for the flight by reviewing weather conditions, flight plans, and other information. During the flight, pilots are responsible for the safe operation of the aircraft, including Navigation, communication with air traffic control, and monitoring the aircraft's systems. After the flight, pilots complete paperwork and debrief with the rest of the crew. This schedule can vary depending on the type of flying and the hours flown.

2. Responsibilities of a Pilot

Pilots are responsible for the safe operation of the aircraft, including Navigation, communication with air traffic control, and monitoring the aircraft's systems. They must also have knowledge of emergency procedures and be able to make quick decisions in case of emergency. Pilots also have to comply with regulations set by the Federal Aviation Administration (FAA) and the airline company.

3. Challenges of a Pilot

Pilots face a variety of challenges, including dealing with unpredictable weather conditions, managing flight plans, and dealing with mechanical issues. They also have to deal with the stress and pressure of flying, as well as the long and irregular hours. In addition, they must maintain their physical and mental fitness and be aware of the risks associated with flying.

4. Conclusion

Being a pilot is an exciting and rewarding career, but it also comes with its own set of responsibilities and challenges. A typical day for a pilot begins well before the flight, as they have to prepare for the flight by reviewing weather conditions, flight plans, and other information. Pilots are responsible for the safe operation of the aircraft, including Navigation, communication with air traffic control, and monitoring the aircraft's systems. The challenges of a pilot include dealing with unpredictable weather conditions, managing flight plans, dealing with mechanical issues, and maintaining physical and mental fitness.

CHAPTER 4:

A Flight from Start to Finish

Becoming a pilot is an exciting and rewarding career, but it's important to understand the responsibilities and tasks that pilots undertake during a flight. In this chapter, we'll take a closer look at what pilots do from the moment they greet the passengers to the final landing.

1. Pre-flight Preparation

Before the flight, pilots undergo a series of

pre-flight preparations. This includes reviewing the flight plan, weather forecast, and aircraft systems, as well as performing a pre-flight inspection of the aircraft. They also check the weight and balance of the aircraft and ensure that all necessary paperwork is in order. Pilots will also review the flight plan, which includes the route, altitude, and flight time, and will check the weather forecast to ensure that the flight can be completed safely. They will also review the aircraft systems to ensure that everything is working properly.

2. Greeting Passengers and Boarding

Once the passengers have boarded the aircraft, pilots greet them and provide a safety briefing. They will explain the location of emergency exits, the use of seat belts, and the use of oxygen masks. They will also provide information about the flight, such as the flight time, route, and weather conditions. Pilots also ensure that all passengers have properly stored their carry-on luggage and that all their seat belts are fastened.

3. Takeoff and Climb

During takeoff, pilots are responsible for controlling the aircraft and ensuring that it takes off safely. They will perform a series of checks, including checking the engine instruments, navigation systems, and radio communications. Once the aircraft is in the air, they will continue to monitor the aircraft systems and ensure that the aircraft is climbing at the correct rate.

4. Cruise and Descent

During the cruise phase of the flight, pilots

will monitor the aircraft systems and ensure that the aircraft is on course. They will also communicate with air traffic control and other aircraft in the area. They will also make any necessary adjustments to the flight plan due to weather or other factors. As the aircraft approaches its destination, pilots will begin the descent and will perform a series of checks, including checking the engine instruments, navigation systems, and radio communications.

5. Landing and Taxiing

During the final approach, pilots will control the aircraft and ensure it lands safely. They will perform a series of checks, including checking the engine instruments, navigation systems, and radio communications. Once the aircraft has landed, pilots will taxi the aircraft to the gate and perform a post-flight inspection.

6. Conclusion

This chapter covers the different tasks and responsibilities that pilots undertake during a flight. From pre-flight preparation, greeting passengers, takeoff and climb, cruise and descent, and landing and taxiing, pilots are responsible for ensuring the safety and smooth operation of the flight. They are responsible for monitoring the aircraft systems, communicating with air traffic control, and making necessary adjustments to the flight plan. They also provide safety briefings and information to passengers and perform inspections before and after the flight. This chapter provides a better understanding of the tasks and responsibilities of pilots and the importance of their role in ensuring a safe and successful flight.

MARTY HODGEF

CHAPTER 5:

The Different Types of Pilots

The aviation industry is made up of a diverse group of pilots whom each play a unique role in keeping the skies safe and the world connected. In this chapter, we will take a closer look at the different types of pilots and the roles they play in the aviation industry.

1. Commercial Airline Pilots

Commercial airline pilots are responsible for flying commercial airliners and transporting passengers and cargo to destinations all over the world. They are highly trained professionals who must pass rigorous training and certification requirements before they can fly for a commercial airline. They work closely with the flight crew, including the co-pilot and flight attendants, to ensure the safety and comfort of their passengers. They also use advanced navigation and communication systems to plan and execute a safe flight. They have to follow strict procedures and regulations set by the Federal Aviation Administration (FAA) and other aviation authorities.

2. Private Pilots

Private pilots fly private aircraft, such as small planes or helicopters. They may be responsible for transporting passengers and cargo or conducting aerial surveys, or other operations. They are also required to pass rigorous training and certification requirements, but the requirements are different from those of commercial pilots. They are not restricted to a specific schedule and can fly for their own pleasure or to conduct business. They can fly to small airports and airfields that commercial airlines cannot reach.

3. Military Pilots

Military pilots are responsible for flying a variety of aircraft, including fighter jets and transport planes, and are responsible for protecting the country's national interests. They go through extensive training and must meet strict physical and mental requirements. They are also required to pass rigorous training and certification requirements. They are trained to fly in various weather conditions, at high altitudes, and in combat situations. They have to be ready for any situation that might arise, including flying in hostile territory and have to be able to make quick decisions under pressure.

4. Air Ambulance Pilots

Air ambulance pilots are responsible for flying medical patients to and from hospitals and other medical facilities. They work closely with medical personnel on board to provide critical care to patients during transport. They are required to have specialized training and certifications in order to operate the medical equipment on board and to fly in a variety of weather and visibility conditions. They must be able to navigate to remote and difficult-to-reach locations and have to be able to make quick decisions in emergency situations.

5. Crop Dusting Pilots

Crop dusting pilots are responsible for applying pesticides and fertilizers to crops from the air. They fly small, specially-designed aircraft that are equipped with tanks and spraying equipment. They must have specialized training and certifications in order to operate the aircraft and equipment safely. They also have to be familiar with the local weather conditions and terrain, as well as the regulations related to crop dusting, to ensure that they are applying the chemicals in a safe and environmentally-friendly manner.

6. Test Pilots

Test pilots are responsible for testing and evaluating new aircraft and aircraft systems before they are put into production or service. They work closely with engineers and designers to identify and resolve any issues with the aircraft. They must have a high level of skill and experience in order to safely test the aircraft in a variety of flight conditions. They are also responsible for providing feedback and recommendations to improve the aircraft's performance and safety.

7. Conclusion

the aviation industry is home to a wide range of pilots whom each play a crucial role in keeping the skies safe and the world connected. From commercial airline pilots to military pilots, each type of pilot has their own set of responsibilities and must meet rigorous training and certification requirements. Each type of pilot requires a specific set of skills and knowledge, and each plays a vital role in the aviation industry.

CHAPTER 6:

The Essential Skills of a Pilot

Being a pilot is an exciting and rewarding career, but it also requires a specific set of skills to be successful. In this chapter, we will take a closer look at some of the key skills required to become a pilot and excel in the aviation industry.

1. Technical Skills

Technical skills are the knowledge and expertise required to operate and navigate an aircraft safely and efficiently. This includes knowledge of aircraft systems, Navigation, meteorology, and air traffic control procedures. Pilots must also have a thorough understanding of the Federal Aviation Regulations (FARs) and other regulations that govern the aviation industry. They need to be able to understand the aircraft's systems and how they work, how to troubleshoot, and how to react when something goes wrong. They should be able to understand the weather conditions and how they affect the flight and the flight plan, and they should know how to communicate with the air traffic control and follow the procedures.

2. Communication Skills

Communication skills are crucial for pilots because they must be able to communicate effectively with air traffic control, other pilots, and the crew. Pilots must also be able to communicate effectively with passengers, providing them with important information about the flight and addressing any concerns they may have. They should be able to convey information clearly and concisely, both verbally and in writing, and be able to understand and respond appropriately to the information received. In case of emergencies, they should be able to remain calm and composed and effectively communicate with other pilots, air traffic controllers, and passengers.

3. Leadership Skills

Leadership skills are essential for pilots because they are the captain of the aircraft and are responsible for the safety and well-being of all passengers and crew on board. This includes making quick and informed decisions in emergency situations and being able to effectively manage and lead the flight crew. A pilot should have the ability to inspire confidence and trust in others, as well as be able to delegate tasks and responsibilities to the flight crew. They should be able to inspire their crew to work together as a team and make sure that everyone is working towards the same goal.

4. Adaptability

Adaptability is important for pilots because they must be able to adapt to different situations and changing conditions while in flight. They should be able to think on their feet, remain calm under pressure and make quick decisions. They should be able to adapt to different weather conditions, flight plans, and unexpected situations. They should also be able to adapt to new technologies and procedures as they are introduced in the aviation industry. This means that they need to be able to learn and adapt quickly and be open to new ideas and changes.

5. Physical and Mental Fitness

Physical and mental fitness are crucial for pilots because they are required to undergo rigorous medical examinations and testing to ensure they are fit to fly. Pilots must also be able to handle the physical and mental demands of long-haul flights, including dealing with jet lag and fatigue. They should have the ability to remain alert and focused during long flights and be able to manage stress and pressure. They should also be able to maintain a healthy lifestyle, which includes regular exercise, a healthy diet, and enough sleep.

6. Conclusion

This chapter covers the key skills required for the job of being a pilot. Technical skills, communication skills, leadership skills, adaptability, and physical and mental fitness are all important for pilots to be successful in the aviation industry. A successful pilot should have the ability to understand and operate the aircraft, communicate effectively, lead and inspire the crew, adapt to changing conditions, and maintain physical and mental fitness. All these skills are crucial to ensure the safety of the passengers and the crew and completing a successful flight.

PART 3: EDUCATION

MARTY HODGEF

CHAPTER 7:

Training and Education

Becoming a pilot is a challenging and rewarding journey that requires a significant investment of time and money. In this chapter, we will take a detailed look at the training and education required to become a pilot, including the types of programs available, the costs involved, and the qualifications and certifications required.

1. Obtaining a Private Pilot's License (PPL)

The first step in becoming a pilot is to obtain a private pilot's license (PPL). This license allows the holder to fly small aircraft for personal and recreational use. To obtain a PPL, a person must be at least 17 years old and must pass a medical examination, as well as complete a certain amount of flight training and pass a written exam and a flight test. Flight training typically takes place at flight schools or with private flight instructors and can be completed in a few months to a year, depending on the individual's schedule and dedication.

2. Further Certifications

After obtaining a PPL, a person can then pursue further certifications, such as a commercial pilot's license (CPL) or an airline transport pilot's license (ATPL). A CPL allows the holder to fly for compensation or hire and requires additional flight hours, as well as passing written and flight exams. An ATPL is the highest level of pilot certification and is required to fly as a captain for a commercial airline. It requires even more flight hours and a more rigorous set of exams.

3. Ground School

In addition to flight training, aspiring pilots must also complete ground school, which includes classroom instruction on topics such as aerodynamics, Navigation, meteorology, and regulations. Ground school can be completed at flight schools or through online or self-study programs.

4. Recurrent Training

Another important aspect of training and education for pilots is recurrent training, which is ongoing training that is required to maintain a pilot's certification. This includes flight hours, simulator training, and other training to stay current and proficient in their skills.

5. Costs Involved

The costs involved in pilot training can vary widely, depending on the type of program and the location. A private pilot's license can cost anywhere from $10,000 to $15,000, while a commercial pilot's license can cost upwards of $50,000. It's important to carefully consider the costs and benefits before embarking on this journey.

6. Conclusion

Becoming a pilot requires a significant investment in terms of time and money. It involves completing flight training, ground school, and passing written and flight exams. Additionally, it's important to have a clear understanding of the costs involved and the time commitment required. But with hard work and dedication, one can achieve the goal of becoming a pilot and have a rewarding career in the aviation industry. The journey starts with obtaining a private pilot's license, followed by further certifications, ground school, recurrent training, and understanding the costs involved. With all these steps, one can become a pilot with a clear understanding of the challenges ahead.

MARTY HODGEF

CHAPTER 8:

Navigation and Flight Planning

Navigation and flight planning are essential skills for pilots as they ensure safe and efficient flights. In this chapter, we will take a closer look at the various navigation and flight planning tools and techniques that pilots use to plan and execute a safe flight.

1. Navigation

Pilots use a variety of navigation tools and techniques to plan and execute a flight. One of the most important tools is the navigation log, which is a detailed plan of the flight route that includes information such as the departure and arrival airports, the route of flight, and the estimated time of arrival. Pilots also use navigation charts, which are detailed maps that show information such as airspace boundaries, radio frequencies, and terrain.

Another important navigation tool is the navigation computer, which is a device that calculates the aircraft's position and provides information such as ground speed, heading, and wind direction. Pilots also use Automatic Dependent Surveillance-Broadcast (ADS-B) systems, which use GPS technology to provide precise location information.

2. Flight Planning

Flight planning is the process of creating a detailed plan for a flight, taking into account factors such as weather, airspace restrictions, and aircraft performance. Pilots use various flight planning tools, such as weather radar and flight planning software, to gather and analyze information and plan the most efficient and safe route for the flight.

Pilots also use performance data to plan a flight, such as the aircraft's weight and balance, fuel consumption, and takeoff and landing distances. This information is used to calculate the aircraft's performance and determine if it is capable of safely completing the flight.

3. Flight Monitoring

During the flight, pilots continuously monitor the aircraft's performance, weather conditions, and other factors to ensure a safe and efficient flight. They use various instruments and systems, such as the flight data recorder and the cockpit voice recorder, to gather and analyze data. They also communicate with air traffic control and other aircraft to ensure safe Navigation and avoid collisions.

4. Conclusion

In summary, Navigation and flight planning are essential skills for pilots as they ensure safe and efficient flights. Pilots use a variety of navigation tools and techniques, such as navigation logs, charts, and computers, as well as flight planning tools, like weather radar and flight planning software, to plan and execute a safe flight. They also continuously monitor the aircraft's performance, weather conditions, and other factors during the flight to ensure safe Navigation and avoid collisions.

CHAPTER 9:

Safety and Emergency Procedures

Safety is of the utmost importance in the aviation industry, and pilots are trained to follow strict procedures to ensure the safety of the passengers and crew. In this chapter, we will take a closer look at the importance of safety in aviation, and the procedures pilots follow in case of an emergency.

1. **Importance of Safety in Aviation**

The aviation industry is one of the safest modes of transportation, and safety is a top priority for pilots, airlines, and aviation authorities. Pilots are trained to follow strict procedures and protocols to ensure the safety of the passengers and crew, and the industry is constantly working to improve safety through advances in technology and training.

Safety is important not only for the passengers and crew but also for the pilots themselves. Pilots are trained to follow strict procedures and protocols to ensure the safety of the passengers and crew, and the industry is constantly working to improve safety through advances in technology and training.

2. Emergency Procedures

Despite the many safety measures in place, emergencies can still occur. Pilots are trained to handle a wide range of emergency situations, including engine failure, power loss, and in-flight fires. They are also trained in emergency communication and evacuation procedures. The crew and pilots also have to be trained to handle medical emergencies that might occur on board.

Pilots also conduct regular emergency drills and simulations to practice and refine their emergency procedures, which helps them to respond quickly and effectively in the event of an emergency.

3. Conclusion

Safety is of the utmost importance in the aviation industry, and pilots are trained to follow strict procedures to ensure the safety of the passengers and crew. Pilots are also trained to handle a wide range of emergency situations, including engine failure, power loss, and in-flight fires, and are also trained in emergency communication and evacuation procedures. Regular emergency drills and simulations help pilots to respond quickly and effectively in the event of an emergency.

CHAPTER 10:

Air Traffic Control and Communication

Communication is a crucial aspect of flying, and pilots rely on air traffic control (ATC) and other aircraft for Navigation and safety. In this chapter, we will take a closer look at how pilots communicate with ATC and other aircraft during a flight.

1. **Air Traffic Control**

Air traffic control (ATC) is responsible for the safe and efficient movement of aircraft in the airspace. Pilots communicate with ATC through radio transmissions, using designated frequencies and procedures. ATC provides pilots with information such as weather conditions, flight plans, and clearance to take off or land. Pilots also receive instructions on altitude, heading, and speed, as well as information on other aircraft in the vicinity.

Pilots are also responsible for maintaining communication with ATC, providing regular updates on their position and flight status, and following ATC instructions to ensure a safe and efficient flight.

2. Communication with other aircraft

Pilots also communicate with other aircraft in the vicinity, using the aircraft's transponder and the Automatic Dependent Surveillance-Broadcast (ADS-B) system. This allows pilots to see the location and flight information of other aircraft in the vicinity, as well as to communicate and coordinate with other aircraft to maintain safe distances and avoid collisions.

In addition, pilots use standard phraseology and procedures when communicating with ATC and other aircraft to ensure clear and accurate communication.

3. Backup communication systems

Pilots also have backup communication systems in case the primary system fails, such as emergency radios and satellite phones. These systems allow pilots to communicate with ATC and other aircraft in the event of an emergency or if the primary communication system fails.

4. Conclusion

Communication is a crucial aspect of flying, and pilots rely on air traffic control (ATC) and other aircraft for Navigation and safety. Pilots communicate with ATC through radio transmissions, using designated frequencies and procedures, and also have to communicate with other aircraft in the vicinity using the aircraft's transponder and the Automatic Dependent Surveillance-Broadcast (ADS-B) system. Pilots also use standard phraseology and procedures when communicating with ATC and other aircraft to ensure clear and accurate communication, and they also have backup communication systems in case the primary system fails.

CHAPTER 11:

Aircraft Systems and Maintenance

Understanding the different systems and components of an aircraft and how they are maintained is crucial for pilots to ensure the safe and efficient operation of the aircraft. In this chapter, we will take a closer look at the various systems and components of an aircraft and the maintenance procedures that are used to ensure their proper functioning.

1. Powerplants and propulsion systems

The powerplants and propulsion systems of an aircraft are responsible for generating the power to move the aircraft. This includes the engines, propellers, and other systems that are used to convert fuel into energy. Pilots must understand the different types of powerplants and propulsion systems, as well as the maintenance procedures that are used to ensure their proper functioning.

2. Electrical systems

The electrical systems of an aircraft are responsible for providing power to the various systems and components of the aircraft. This includes the battery, generators, and other systems that are used to generate and distribute electrical power. Pilots must understand the different types of electrical systems and the maintenance procedures that are used to ensure their proper functioning.

3. Flight control systems

The flight control systems of an aircraft are responsible for controlling the movement of the aircraft. This includes the rudder, ailerons, elevators, and other systems that are used to control the aircraft's altitude, speed, and direction. Pilots must understand the different types of flight control systems and the maintenance procedures that are used to ensure their proper functioning.

4. Maintenance procedures

Regular maintenance is crucial for ensuring the safe and efficient operation of an aircraft. Pilots must understand the various maintenance procedures that are used to keep the aircraft in good working order. This includes inspections, repairs, and replacements of various systems and components, as well as the use of specialized tools and equipment.

5. Conclusion

Understanding the different systems and components of an aircraft and how they are maintained is crucial for pilots to ensure the safe and efficient operation of the aircraft. This includes understanding the power plants and propulsion systems, electrical systems, flight control systems, and regular maintenance procedures that are used to keep the aircraft in good working order. It's essential for pilots to have a solid understanding of these systems and how to maintain them to ensure the safety of the passengers and crew, as well as the aircraft's overall performance.

PART 4: CAREER

MARTY HODGEF

CHAPTER 12:

From School to Skies

Pursuing a career in aviation can be an exciting and fulfilling path, but it's important to be prepared for the education and training that's required. In this chapter, we'll take a closer look at the subjects that are recommended for students who are interested in a career in aviation.

1. Math and Physics

Math and physics are essential subjects for anyone interested in a career in aviation. These subjects provide a strong foundation in the principles of aerodynamics, Navigation, and aircraft systems. A good understanding of math and physics will be useful for understanding the technical aspects of flying and aircraft design. Math, specifically, will be useful for understanding the calculations that are required for Navigation and flight planning. Physics, on the other hand, will be useful for understanding the principles of aerodynamics and how the aircraft works. You will learn about the physics of lift, drag, thrust, and weight and how they relate to the aircraft's performance.

2. English and Communication

English and communication are important subjects for pilots because they must be able to communicate effectively with air traffic control, other pilots, and the crew. English is also the international language of aviation, and pilots must be able to communicate effectively in both written and spoken English. Good communication skills are necessary for pilots as they need to be able to convey information clearly and concisely, both verbally and in writing. They should also be able to understand and respond appropriately to the information received. Effective communication is crucial for pilots, as it can ensure the safety of the flight and the comfort of the passengers.

3. Computer Science

Computer science is an important subject for pilots because modern aircraft are increasingly reliant on computer systems. A good understanding of computer science will be useful for understanding the Navigation, weather radar, and flight control systems of modern aircraft. Computer science is also important for pilots as they need to be able to understand the computer systems that are used in the cockpit. They need to be able to troubleshoot any issues that might arise and be able to use the navigation systems and weather radar effectively.

4. Economics

Economics is an important subject for pilots because it provides an understanding of the aviation industry and the business aspects of running an airline. Understanding economics will be useful for understanding the financial aspects of the aviation industry and the factors that influence airfares and flight schedules. Economics is important for pilots as they need to understand the business aspects of the aviation industry. They should have a good understanding of how airlines operate and how to manage the economic aspects of a flight. They should also be able to understand the market dynamics and how it affects the aviation industry. They should also be able to understand the concepts of supply and demand and how they affect airfares and flight schedules.

5. Meteorology

Meteorology is an important subject for pilots because it provides an understanding of the weather conditions that affect flights. Pilots must be able to understand and interpret weather forecasts and understand the effects of weather on flight planning and aircraft performance. Meteorology is important for pilots as they need to be able to understand the weather conditions that affect their flights. They need to be able to interpret weather forecasts and understand how the weather will affect their flight plan. They should also be able to understand how different weather conditions will affect the aircraft's performance and how to react to them.

6. Conclusion

This chapter covers the recommended subjects for students interested in a career in aviation. Math and physics, English and communication, computer science, economics, and meteorology are all important subjects for students to consider in order to be well-prepared for a career in aviation. These subjects provide a strong foundation in the technical, communication, computer, business, and weather aspects of the aviation industry. By mastering these subjects, students will be well-prepared for the education and training that is required to become successful pilots.

CHAPTER 13:

Careers in Aviation

The aviation industry offers a wide range of career paths, from commercial to military and private flying. In this chapter, we will take a closer look at the different career paths available in aviation and the qualifications and requirements for each.

1. Commercial Flying

Commercial flying is one of the most popular career paths in aviation and includes working as a pilot for an airline, cargo carrier, or corporate flight department. To become a commercial pilot, one must have a commercial pilot's license (CPL) and must meet the minimum flight hour requirements set by the Federal Aviation Administration (FAA). In addition, commercial pilots must pass a rigorous set of written and flight exams and must meet the medical and physical requirements set by the FAA.

2. Military Flying

Military flying is another popular career path in aviation and includes working as a pilot for the Air Force, Navy, Army, or Coast Guard. To become a military pilot, one must meet the qualifications and requirements set by the military branch they are interested in joining. This typically includes a bachelor's degree, passing a series of physical and psychological tests, and completing officer training. Military pilots must also pass a rigorous set of flight exams and meet the medical and physical requirements set by the military.

3. Private Flying

Private flying is the third most popular career path in aviation and includes working as a private pilot, flight instructor, or charter pilot. To become a private pilot, one must have a private pilot's license (PPL) and must meet the minimum flight hour requirements set by the FAA. Private pilots must also pass a written exam and a flight test and must meet the medical and physical requirements set by the FAA.

4. Conclusion

The aviation industry offers a wide range of career paths, from commercial to military and private flying. Each career path has its own qualifications and requirements, such as a commercial pilot's license (CPL) for commercial flying, meeting qualifications and requirements set by a military branch for military flying, and a private pilot's license (PPL) for private flying. In addition, all pilots must pass written and flight exams and meet medical and physical requirements set by the appropriate regulatory agency (FAA or military). It's important for individuals interested in a career in aviation to research and understand the qualifications and requirements for the specific career path they are interested in pursuing in order to make an informed decision and successfully navigate the path to their desired aviation career.

CHAPTER 14:

The Rewards

Becoming a pilot is a challenging and rewarding career, but what do pilots like most about their job? In this chapter, we'll take a look at some of the things that pilots find most enjoyable and rewarding about their profession.

1. The Thrill of Flight

One of the things that pilots enjoy most about their job is the thrill of flight. Pilots have the opportunity to experience the sensation of soaring through the skies, taking in the stunning views, and feeling the power of the aircraft beneath them. The feeling of being in control of such a powerful machine is an exhilarating experience, and pilots often say that the thrill of flying is what keeps them coming back to the job.

2. The Sense of Adventure

Another thing that pilots enjoy about their job is the sense of adventure that comes with it. Pilots have the opportunity to travel to different parts of the world and experience new cultures and landscapes. They also get to meet new people and connect with people from all over the world. The adventure of traveling and the opportunity to experience new things is something that many pilots find very rewarding.

3. The Sense of Responsibility

Pilots take on a lot of responsibility, and many pilots find this to be one of the most enjoyable parts of their job. They are responsible for the safety of hundreds of passengers, and they take this responsibility very seriously. Pilots also take pride in the fact that they are responsible for getting passengers to their destinations safely and on time.

4. The Sense of Accomplishment

Pilots often find that they get a great sense of accomplishment from their job. When they successfully fly a plane full of passengers to their destination, they feel a sense of pride and accomplishment. They also enjoy the challenge of working with their crew to solve problems and find that their ability to handle difficult situations is something that they take pride in.

5. The Camaraderie

Pilots often form close bonds with their colleagues, and many pilots find that the camaraderie among pilots is one of the most enjoyable parts of their job. They work together as a team, and they support each other through the challenges of the job. They also enjoy the opportunity to share their experiences and knowledge with other pilots.

6. Conclusion

This chapter covers some of the things that pilots enjoy most about their job. They enjoy the thrill of flight, the sense of adventure, the sense of responsibility, the sense of accomplishment, and the camaraderie among pilots. They also appreciate the opportunity to travel and experience new things and form bonds with colleagues. Overall, pilots find that the combination of these rewarding aspects of the job makes it an exciting and fulfilling career choice.

MARTY HODGEF

CHAPTER 15:

The Challenges

Becoming a pilot is a challenging and rewarding career, but it's not without its downsides. In this chapter, we'll take a look at some of the things that pilots find most difficult and least enjoyable about their profession.

1. Long Working Hours

One of the things that pilots often find difficult about their job is the long working hours. Pilots are often required to work long shifts and be away from home for extended periods of time. This can be hard on pilots, as well as their families. Pilots also often have to work on holidays and weekends, which can make it difficult to have a good work-life balance.

2. Jet Lag and Fatigue

Another thing that pilots find difficult is dealing with jet lag and fatigue. Pilots often have to fly across different time zones, which can cause jet lag and fatigue. This can make it difficult to stay alert and focused during the flight, which can be dangerous. Pilots also have to deal with the fatigue that comes with working long hours and being away from home.

3. Stress and Pressure

Pilots are often under a lot of stress and pressure, and many pilots find this to be one of the most difficult parts of their job.

They are responsible for the safety of hundreds of passengers, and they take this responsibility very seriously. Pilots also have to deal with the stress and pressure of working with a tight schedule, which can be very demanding.

4. Weather-Related Delays

Pilots often have to deal with weather-related delays, which can be frustrating and difficult. Pilots have to make sure that the flight is safe, which can mean that flights are delayed or even canceled. Pilots also have to deal with the stress and pressure of trying to get passengers to their destination on time, even when there are weather-related delays.

5. The Risk of Injury or Death

Pilots also have to deal with the risk of injury or death, which can be difficult to accept. Pilots are trained to handle a wide range of emergency situations, but even with the best training, there is still a risk of injury or death. Pilots also have to deal with the stress and pressure of knowing that they are responsible for the safety of hundreds of passengers.

6. Conclusion

This chapter covers some of the things that pilots don't like most about their job. They often find the long working hours, jet lag and fatigue, stress and pressure, weather-related delays, and the risk of injury or death as the most challenging aspects of their job. These factors can make the job demanding and difficult and can make it hard to maintain a good work-life balance. Despite these challenges, pilots continue to find the job rewarding and fulfilling. They take pride in their role in ensuring the safety of passengers and in their ability to handle the challenges that come with the job. Pilots are also trained to handle difficult situations and to manage the stress and pressure that comes with the job.

MARTY HODGEF

CHAPTER 16:

Tips for Success

A career in aviation can be challenging and competitive, but with the right strategies and mindset, one can achieve success. In this chapter, we will take a closer look at some of the key strategies for achieving success in an aviation career, including networking, perseverance, and continuous learning.

1. Networking

Networking is an important aspect of any career, and the aviation industry is no exception. Building relationships with other professionals in the industry can help open doors to new opportunities and provide valuable information and support throughout one's career. Pilots should take advantage of opportunities to meet and connect with other professionals in the industry through networking events, industry organizations, and online communities.

2. Perseverance

Perseverance is key to achieving success in an aviation career. The path to becoming a pilot can be long and challenging, and there will be obstacles and setbacks along the way. It's essential to have the determination and grit to persist in the face of challenges and to never give up on one's goals.

3. Continuous Learning

The aviation industry is constantly evolving and changing, and pilots must be willing to continuously learn and adapt to stay current and competitive. This includes staying current with new technologies and regulations, as well as expanding one's knowledge and skills through additional training and education.

4. Conclusion

A career in aviation can be challenging and competitive, but with the right strategies and mindset, one can achieve success. Networking, perseverance, and continuous learning are key strategies for achieving success in an aviation career. Building relationships with other professionals in the industry, having the determination and grit to persist in the face of challenges, and staying current with new technologies and regulations are important aspects to have in order to have a successful career in aviation.

MARTY HODGEF

CONCLUSION

In this book, we have explored the exciting world of aviation and the steps it takes to become a pilot. From the history of aviation to the different types of pilots, training and education, and the life of a pilot, we have covered a wide range of topics that are essential for anyone interested in pursuing a career in aviation. We have also discussed the importance of safety, emergency procedures, air traffic control and communication, aircraft systems and maintenance, and careers in aviation.

The key takeaway from this book is that becoming a pilot takes dedication, hard work, and a passion for aviation. It is not an easy path, but with perseverance, the right training and education, and a commitment to safety and continuous learning, anyone can achieve their dream of becoming a pilot.

We hope that this book has provided valuable information and inspiration for young readers who are interested in pursuing a career in aviation. We encourage you to follow your dreams and never give up on your goals. The aviation industry is constantly changing and offers a wide range of career opportunities, and with the right mindset, attitude, and training, you can become a successful pilot.

In conclusion, this book has aimed to give a comprehensive overview of what it takes to become a pilot and how to achieve success in an aviation career. We hope that it has been informative and inspiring for young readers who are interested in pursuing a career in aviation, and we encourage them to follow their dreams and work hard to achieve their goals.

MARTY HODGEF

Made in the USA
Columbia, SC
02 October 2023